P9-AFS-904

HOW POLITICAL PARTIES WORK

by Stephanie Finne

Content Consultant
Dr. Arnold Shober
Associate Professor of Government
Lawrence University

Core Library

An Imprint of Abdo Publishing
www.abdopublishing.com

www.abdopublishing.com

Published by Abdo Publishing, a division of ABDO, PO Box 398166, Minneapolis,
Minnesota 55439. Copyright © 2015 by Abdo Consulting Group, Inc. International
copyrights reserved in all countries. No part of this book may be reproduced in any form
without written permission from the publisher. Core Library™ is a trademark and logo of
Abdo Publishing.

Printed in the United States of America, North Mankato, Minnesota
102014
012015

Cover Photo: iStockphoto
Interior Photos: iStockphoto, 1, 34; Pablo Martinez Monsivais/AP Images, 4; Charlie
Neibergall/AP Images, 6; Red Line Editorial, 7, 37; Stacy Thacker/AP Images, 9, 45; US
National Archives and Records Administration, 12; North Wind Picture Archives, 14;
Library of Congress, 17; Ralph Eleaser Whiteside Earl, 20; Justin Sullivan/Thinkstock,
22; William G. Jackman/Library of Congress, 25; AP Images, 29; Charles Dharapak/AP
Images, 30; Mary Altaffer/AP Images, 39; Carolyn Kaster/AP Images, 40

Editor: Heather C. Hudak
Series Designer: Becky Daum

Library of Congress Control Number: 2014944214

Cataloging-in-Publication Data
Finne, Stephanie.
 How political parties work / Stephanie Finne.
   p. cm. -- (How the US government works)
ISBN 978-1-62403-634-7 (lib. bdg.)
Includes bibliographical references and index.
1. Political parties--United States--Juvenile literature. 2. Political campaigns--United
States--Juvenile literature. 3. United States--Politics and government--Juvenile literature.
I. Title.
324--dc23

                                                    2014944214

CONTENTS

CHAPTER ONE

Party Support

It was a cold night in November 2012. More than 20,000 people braved the chilly weather in Des Moines, Iowa. They stood outside for hours and listened to speeches in support of Barack Obama, the president of the United States. This was the final political rally for Obama before the next day's presidential election. Obama and his Democratic supporters hoped the president would be reelected.

President Barack Obama spoke to his supporters on November 5, 2012, in Des Moines, Iowa.

Rock musician Bruce Springsteen performed at Obama's final campaign rally before the 2012 election.

US flags waved in the breeze as people held up signs supporting the president. Obama's aides spoke of the long road to his first-term win in 2008. Four years earlier, the president's campaign had held similar political rallies all across the country. Rallies are held to urge voters to elect a specific person to a public office, such as the presidency. The rallies urged voters to elect Obama as president.

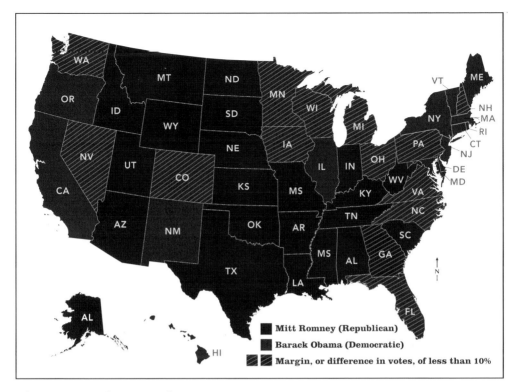

Mitt Romney (Republican)

Barack Obama (Democratic)

Margin, or difference in votes, of less than 10%

The 2012 Election by State

This map shows which political parties' candidates people voted for in the 2012 presidential election. Are you surprised by how the states voted? How does this map help you understand US political parties?

But to win the presidency, Obama needed the support of the Democratic Party, one of the two major political parties in the United States. Months before, the Democratic Party had decided to stand behind Obama during his run for the presidency. The party helped him pay for his campaign and organize rallies across the country. Well-known members of the party, including former president Bill Clinton, spoke in support of Obama.

On November 6, 2012, the nation learned the Democrats' hard work and support had paid off. Obama had been reelected to serve a second term as president of the United States.

What Is a Political Party?

The Democratic Party is just one of many political parties in the United States. Political parties are organizations of people with similar beliefs and political ideas. People in a political party work together to achieve common goals. Most political parties have a platform. This is a statement explaining the party's goals, strategies, and principles. Some political parties have millions of members. Other parties are much smaller.

Political parties help influence laws, elect leaders, and inform citizens about major issues. The party system plays an important role in the US government.

Reince Priebus, a leader in the Republican Party, spoke at a Republican meeting in 2014 in preparation for the 2016 presidential election.

Two Main Parties

The United States has a two-party system. That means it has two main political parties. The Democratic Party is one. The Republican Party is the other. Since the modern party system was established in 1860, every US president has come from either the Republican

Forming a Majority

The party with the most members in the legislature is called the majority party. The party with the fewest members is called the minority party. The majority party elects the leadership in each house of Congress. The majority party has the most influence in each house, but the minority party also has an important job. It can slow down or even stop laws from being passed by the majority party.

or Democratic Parties. However, the United States also has dozens of smaller political parties.

Voters Choose

The United States is a democracy. This means US citizens elect the people who will run the country. Voters elect the president and vice president. They also elect members of Congress, which is the legislative branch of the government. Congress makes the nation's laws.

Congress is divided into two houses: the House of Representatives and the Senate. Voters elect members to both houses. Voters also cast ballots for state officials, governors, mayors, and judges.

Congress members and other elected officials are almost always associated with a political party. Elected officials will usually consider their party's platform when making decisions.

FURTHER EVIDENCE

Chapter One introduced you to the two major political parties in the United States. Identify one of the chapter's main points. What evidence does the author provide to support this point? The website at the link below also discusses the US political party system. Find a quote on this website that supports the main point you identified. Does the quote support an existing piece of evidence in the chapter? Or does it offer a new piece of evidence?

US Political Parties
www.mycorelibrary.com/political-parties

We the People

of the United States, in order to form a more perfect Union, insure domestic Tranquility, provide for the common defence, promote the general Welfare, and secure the Blessings of Liberty to ourselves and our Posterity, do ordain and establish this Constitution for the United States of America.

Article. I.

Section. 1. All legislative Powers herein granted shall be vested in a Congress of the United States, which shall consist of a Senate and House of Representatives.

Section. 2. The House of Representatives shall be composed of Members chosen every second Year by the People of the several States, and the Electors in each State shall have the Qualifications requisite for Electors of the most numerous Branch of the State Legislature.

No Person shall be a Representative who shall not have attained to the Age of twenty five Years, and been seven Years a Citizen of the United States, and who shall not, when elected, be an Inhabitant of that State in which he shall be chosen.

Representatives and direct Taxes shall be apportioned among the several States which may be included within this Union, according to their respective Numbers, which shall be determined by adding to the whole Number of free Persons, including those bound to Service for a Term of Years, and excluding Indians not taxed, three fifths of all other Persons. The actual Enumeration shall be made within three Years after the first Meeting of the Congress of the United States, and within every subsequent Term of ten Years, in such Manner as they shall by Law direct. The Number of Representatives shall not exceed one for every thirty Thousand, but each State shall have at Least one Representative; and until such enumeration shall be made, the State of New Hampshire shall be entitled to chuse three, Massachusetts eight, Rhode Island and Providence Plantations one, Connecticut five, New York six, New Jersey four, Pennsylvania eight, Delaware one, Maryland six, Virginia ten, North Carolina five, South Carolina five, and Georgia three.

When vacancies happen in the Representation from any State, the Executive Authority thereof shall issue Writs of Election to fill such Vacancies.

The House of Representatives shall chuse their Speaker and other Officers; and shall have the sole Power of Impeachment.

Section. 3. The Senate of the United States shall be composed of two Senators from each State, chosen by the Legislature thereof, for six Years; and each Senator shall have one Vote.

Immediately after they shall be assembled in Consequence of the first Election, they shall be divided as equally as may be into three Classes. The Seats of the Senators of the first Class shall be vacated at the Expiration of the second Year, of the second Class at the Expiration of the fourth Year, and of the third Class at the Expiration of the sixth Year, so that one third may be chosen every second Year; and if Vacancies happen by Resignation, or otherwise, during the Recess of the Legislature of any State, the Executive thereof may make temporary Appointments until the next Meeting of the Legislature, which shall then fill such Vacancies.

No Person shall be a Senator who shall not have attained to the Age of thirty Years, and been nine Years a Citizen of the United States, and who shall not, when elected, be an Inhabitant of that State for which he shall be chosen.

The Vice President of the United States shall be President of the Senate, but shall have no Vote, unless they be equally divided.

The Senate shall chuse their other Officers, and also a President pro tempore, in the Absence of the Vice President, or when he shall exercise the Office of President of the United States.

The Senate shall have the sole Power to try all Impeachments. When sitting for that Purpose, they shall be on Oath or Affirmation. When the President of the United States is tried, the Chief Justice shall preside: And no Person shall be convicted without the Concurrence of two thirds of the Members present.

Judgment in Cases of Impeachment shall not extend further than to removal from Office, and disqualification to hold and enjoy any Office of honor, Trust or Profit under the United States: but the Party convicted shall nevertheless be liable and subject to Indictment, Trial, Judgment and Punishment, according to Law.

Section. 4. The Times, Places and Manner of holding Elections for Senators and Representatives, shall be prescribed in each State by the Legislature thereof; but the Congress may at any time by Law make or alter such Regulations, except as to the Places of chusing Senators.

The Congress shall assemble at least once in every Year, and such Meeting shall be on the first Monday in December, unless they shall by Law appoint a different Day.

Section. 5. Each House shall be the Judge of the Elections, Returns and Qualifications of its own Members, and a Majority of each shall constitute a Quorum to do Business; but a smaller Number may adjourn from day to day, and may be authorized to compel the Attendance of absent Members, in such Manner, and under such Penalties as each House may provide.

Each House may determine the Rules of its Proceedings, punish its Members for disorderly Behaviour, and, with the Concurrence of two thirds, expel a Member.

Each House shall keep a Journal of its Proceedings, and from time to time publish the same, excepting such Parts as may in their Judgment require Secrecy; and the Yeas and Nays of the Members of either House on any question shall, at the Desire of one fifth of those Present, be entered on the Journal.

Neither House, during the Session of Congress, shall, without the Consent of the other, adjourn for more than three days, nor to any other Place than that in which the two Houses shall be sitting.

Section. 6. The Senators and Representatives shall receive a Compensation for their Services, to be ascertained by Law, and paid out of the Treasury of the United States. They shall in all Cases, except Treason, Felony and Breach of the Peace, be privileged from Arrest during their Attendance at the Session of their respective Houses, and in going to and returning from the same; and for any Speech or Debate in either House, they shall not be questioned in any other Place.

No Senator or Representative shall, during the Time for which he was elected, be appointed to any civil Office under the Authority of the United States, which shall have been created, or the Emoluments whereof shall have been encreased during such time; and no Person holding any Office under the United States, shall be a Member of either House during his Continuance in Office.

CHAPTER TWO

Parties of the Past

The US government has one of the oldest political party systems in the world. However, political parties were not a part of the early United States. In fact, the Constitution, the document that established how the US government would function, doesn't mention political parties at all.

The Constitution established a framework of laws for the United States.

In 1787, a group of US leaders met to set up the new US system of government.

Building a Government

The United States began as 13 colonies of Great Britain. Many colonists, however, thought the colonies should be an independent nation. From 1775 to 1783, the colonists fought for independence in the American Revolutionary War. The British surrendered in 1783. US leaders faced the enormous task of developing a government for the young country.

In 1787 a group of US leaders representing each of the 13 colonies met in Philadelphia, Pennsylvania. Their meeting was known as the Constitutional Convention. The document they developed, the US Constitution, provided the framework for the country's government. It included a federal government with legislative, executive, and judicial branches. Each branch limited the power of the other branches. This would prevent any one branch from becoming too powerful.

Those who agreed with the Constitution's call to form a central government were called Federalists. Those who were against creating a central government were called Anti-Federalists. The two groups argued strongly for their beliefs. In the end, support for the Federalists' central government won. The Constitution was ratified, or passed, in 1788.

The First Party

In 1789 the nation's first president, George Washington, appointed Alexander Hamilton as the first US Secretary of the Treasury. Hamilton would lead the department in charge of the country's finances. Hamilton wanted a strong central government. He and his supporters formed the Federalist Party, the first political party in the United States, in 1791.

The Federalist Party believed the government should pay debts from the American Revolutionary War. The party wanted to create a central bank run by the government. It also wanted to remain neutral in wars between foreign countries while maintaining a strong national defense. The party supported establishing a positive relationship with Great Britain.

The Democratic-Republican Party

Although the Federalist Party had a lot of support, many Americans disagreed with the party's ideas. Secretary of State Thomas Jefferson was especially opposed to Hamilton's desire for strong government

Alexander Hamilton led the Federalist Party, which was the first US political party.

influence in the economy. In 1792 Jefferson's supporters united to become the Republican Party. They eventually became known as the Democratic-Republicans. This party believed in a smaller central government. It wanted less control of federal money and a smaller military. Its members believed states should be able to govern themselves with little or no interference from the federal government.

By the time Jefferson was elected president in 1801, Democratic-Republican ideas were gaining popularity. Presidents James Madison and James Monroe were also Democratic-Republicans. They overturned some of the Federalist policies. They reduced the size of the US armed forces and the national debt.

The Federalist Party never held power again after the election of 1801. By the 1820s, the party no longer existed. A new party that supported Federalist economic principles was formed in 1854. The party's members called themselves Republicans. The Republican Party continues to exist today.

A Party Splits

The Democratic-Republican Party slowly drifted apart after its creation. After the election of 1824, it split in two. One group became the Whig Party. The other group kept the name and ideals of the Democratic-Republican Party.

The Whig Party was led by former President John Quincy Adams, who had been president from 1825 to 1829. The party was active from 1834 to 1854. It opposed the way Democratic-Republican President Andrew Jackson governed the country. It claimed Jackson had too much power and acted as a king instead of a president. The Whig Party never developed a firm platform, but several members were elected president.

After the Whigs split off into their own party,

Liberals and Conservatives

In the United States, the terms *liberal* and *conservative* refer to opposite ends of the political spectrum. Liberals usually believe the government should protect equal rights for all individuals. Liberals also believe the government should ensure no one is in need. They often support government programs that provide financial assistance and health care to those who can't afford it. Conservatives tend to believe in limited government. They think people should take care of themselves. They often oppose legislation that limits personal freedom. The modern Democratic Party tends to follow liberal beliefs. The modern Republican Party tends to follow conservative beliefs.

Andrew Jackson is considered the first Democratic Party president of the United States.

the Democratic-Republican Party continued to focus on local concerns and the rights of individual states. Soon it dropped the Republican part of its name. By 1844 it was officially known as the Democratic Party. This party still exists today.

The first president of the United States, George Washington, did not belong to a political party. In fact he warned US citizens against political parties in his 1796 Farewell Address. He said:

> In contemplating the causes which may disturb our Union, it occurs as matter of serious concern that any ground should have been furnished for characterizing parties by geographical discriminations, Northern and Southern, Atlantic and Western; whence designing men may endeavor to excite a belief that there is a real difference of local interests and views. One of the expedients of party to acquire influence within particular districts is to misrepresent the opinions and aims of other districts. You cannot shield yourselves too much against the jealousies and heartburnings which spring from these misrepresentations; they tend to render alien to each other those who ought to be bound together by fraternal affection.

Source: George Washington. "Washington's Farewell Address, 1796." Yale Law School. Lillian Goldman Law Library, 2008. Web. Accessed May 15, 2014.

Back It Up

Why does Washington feel political parties are a bad idea? Write a paragraph describing his main point. Then write down two or three pieces of evidence he uses to make the point.

CHAPTER THREE

The US Parties

Both of the main US political parties formed more than 100 years ago. Both parties have undergone major changes since then. Issues such as slavery, the nation's expansion, and states' rights helped form each party's current platform. Issues such as same-sex marriage, welfare programs, and foreign policy continue to divide the two parties.

Presidential candidate Mitt Romney greets fellow Republicans at a rally in 2012.

The Republican Party

The Republican Party quickly grew in popularity after its formation in 1854. One of the main issues in the party's platform was slavery. At the time, slavery was legal in Southern states but illegal in Northern states. As Americans began spreading out across the continent, new states formed. Some Republicans thought slavery should be banned in the new states. The party eventually worked to end slavery altogether following the American Civil War (1861–1865).

Early Republicans wanted a strong federal government with authority over state governments. They also wanted to provide federal support for middle-class citizens. They passed laws that were friendly to businesses. The party supported railroads and interstate trade. Republican leaders also passed laws giving free land to settlers willing to build houses and farms. The party supported government funding for freed slaves, civil rights for African Americans, and state-supported higher education. Most Republicans

Republican President Abraham Lincoln led the United States during the Civil War, but he did not live to see his country reunited. The president was murdered on April 15, 1865.

were Northern businessmen, farmers, and other workers.

Republican Party ideals changed over time. Republicans eventually supported a more limited government. They thought it should be less involved

Party Symbols

The Republican Party goes by many names. It is called the Grand Old Party, or GOP, and sometimes the Party of Lincoln. Its symbol is an elephant, which represents strength. The Republican Party is usually represented by the color red. The Democratic Party calls itself the "Party of the People." Its symbol is the donkey. Some say this is because in 1828, Andrew Jackson decided to use the strong-willed animal on his campaign posters. Though often used to represent the party, the party has never officially accepted the donkey as its symbol. The Democratic Party is usually represented by the color blue.

in the day-to-day running of the country. This idea holds true today.

Today's Republicans are typically in favor of lower taxes. The party opposes increases in government welfare programs that assist people with low incomes.

Today's Republicans believe the best decisions are made by individuals, not the government. They think businesses and the US economy should be free to operate without government interference.

The Democratic Party

After the American Civil War, Democrats were against equal rights for African Americans. They supported laws that enforced separation between African Americans and whites. They also agreed with laws that prevented African Americans from voting. During this time, Democrats supported local government. They were opposed to taxes and federal government activity.

In the early 1900s, however, the Democratic Party began to change. It shifted toward more liberal ideas, such as more involvement by the federal government in the economy and Americans' daily lives. But in the 1920s, the US economy was booming. Many people agreed with Republicans that the government should play a smaller role in overseeing the US economy. Republicans won all three presidential elections in the 1920s.

During the 1930s, the United States was experiencing an economic hardship known as the

Great Depression. Millions of Americans were unemployed. Banks closed. People struggled to afford basic needs such as food, clothing, and shelter. The Democratic Party's Franklin D. Roosevelt was elected president in 1932. He created many government programs, known collectively as the New Deal, to help Americans protect their savings and find jobs.

Many Americans felt Roosevelt got the country out of the Great Depression. Under Roosevelt's leadership, the Democratic Party became the most popular party in the country. It continued supporting the idea of a strong federal government. The party also began supporting equal rights for all Americans. During the civil rights movement of the 1950s and 1960s, many Democrats fought for equal rights for African Americans.

The modern Democratic Party believes the government should help care for the poor, unemployed, and elderly. The party supports government efforts to provide health care and

Democratic Party President Franklin D. Roosevelt, seated, helped pass many laws giving assistance to unemployed Americans.

In March 2010, Democratic Party president Barack Obama signed an important health care law.

education for all US citizens. It sometimes votes for higher taxes to pay for programs supporting these goals. The party is in favor of the government having strict rules for businesses and industry.

Most Democrats also support equal rights, such as same-sex marriage.

Other Parties

The Democratic and Republican Parties are not the only parties in the United States. The United States has many smaller political parties as well. Some of the best-known smaller political parties include the Libertarian Party, the Reform Party, and the Green Party.

The Libertarian Party is the third-largest party in the United States. Its members believe in an extremely limited government with few powers. The Reform Party's platform focuses mainly on economic issues. Its members believe the United States should work hard to lower the national debt. The Green Party focuses on environmental issues. Its members want to create a new society that balances nature and communities. It also supports equal rights for all US citizens.

The Tea Party

The Tea Party is not registered as an official party. However, this group has still played a major role in several elections since 2009. Tea Party members want to limit the size and reach of the central government. They also want to reduce government spending and eliminate taxes. Tea Party members typically support Republican candidates.

The US electoral process requires a majority of votes to win. This makes it difficult for smaller parties to win presidential elections. However, candidates from smaller parties are occasionally elected to other government positions. This allows them to work on passing laws that promote their party's platform.

The following is an excerpt from the Republican Party platform of 1860, published one year before the start of the American Civil War:

> 8. That the normal condition of all the territory of the United States is that of freedom: That, as our Republican fathers, when they had abolished slavery in all our national territory, ordained that "no persons should be deprived of life, liberty or property without due process of law," it becomes our duty, by legislation, whenever such legislation is necessary, to maintain this provision of the Constitution against all attempts to violate it; and we deny the authority of Congress, of a territorial legislature, or of any individuals, to give legal existence to slavery in any territory of the United States.

Source: "1860 Republican Party Platform." The American Presidency Project. University of California, Santa Barbara, 2014. Web. Accessed September 22, 2014.

What's the Big Idea?

Take a close look at this part of the platform. How does its writer argue for the party's beliefs? How was this commitment tested during the American Civil War?

Political Parties at Work

Political parties form when groups of people with the same opinions join together. First the people must decide the party's platform. They also choose its name, symbol, and slogan. The party's members talk to other people about the platform, trying to gain more members. The party tries to get its members elected to government positions.

Political parties play an important role in helping voters decide which candidate to vote for.

Elections

General elections are held the Tuesday after the first Monday in November. Mayors, judges, and other officials may be up for election. Members of Congress are elected in even-numbered years. The president and vice president are elected every four years. US citizens must be 18 years or older to vote. But there are other ways for young people to get involved in politics. Volunteering for a political party or on a political campaign is a great way to find out more about how government works.

Voting by Party

Political parties help voters decide which candidates to support. Citizens vote for the person and party they believe will best represent their views and needs in office. Voters who agree with a party's platform usually support the party. For most voters, political parties also represent a set of ideals. Many people don't agree with 100 percent of their party's platform.

Approximately 60 percent of US citizens are strong supporters of a particular party. They almost always vote for candidates that belong to their

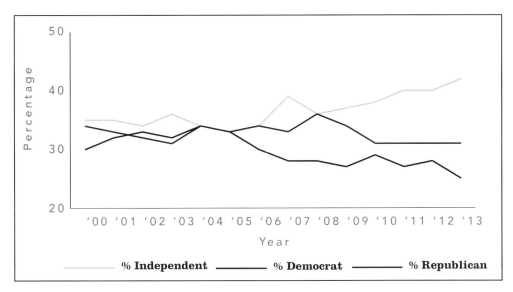

Voters by Party

This graph shows which party voters identified themselves with between 2000 and 2013. How does the information relate to the text about political parties? Do the figures match the information you read? Were you surprised by the information?

preferred party. About 40 percent of voters do not support a specific party. They are called independent voters. They make voting decisions based on the candidates and their beliefs about certain issues. Approximately 40 percent of independent voters tend to support the Republican Party. About 40 percent lean toward the Democratic Party. But these voters may be persuaded to vote for the opposite party if they prefer that party's candidate.

Choosing a Candidate

The Democratic and Republican parties each hold a national convention before every presidential election. At this meeting, the party's members vote for the candidate they believe has the greatest chance of being elected. Each party supports only one presidential candidate. After the candidate is chosen, the party campaigns to get that person elected. It holds rallies, fundraisers, and debates. The party may also pay for commercials and other ads supporting the candidate.

Political parties try hard to convince independent voters to vote for their candidate. The parties know the more members they elect, the easier it will be for their party to pass laws.

Party Roles in the Government

Political parties inform US citizens about important issues. Each party takes a stand on an issue and argues with other parties when they disagree. These party debates help citizens learn about the pros and cons of different issues.

Republican Paul Ryan spoke at the Republican National Convention in 2012.

Political parties help keep the government balanced. The minority party can keep the majority party from taking complete control. Party leaders can criticize the majority power's actions and keep them from gaining too much power.

A group of Democratic US Congress members spoke in favor of a bill that would change US immigration law on the steps of the US Capitol in 2014.

Federal and state legislators support their party's positions when reviewing laws and policies. Elected officials are expected to use the platform as a guide for their actions. They usually vote according to their party's platform.

The United States has many political parties, both large and small. No matter their size, political parties have played a part in nearly every election in the country's history. They will be an important part of US government for many years to come.

EXPLORE ONLINE

Chapter Four discusses political parties and how they can affect voting and elections. The website at the link below also discusses elections. As you know, every source is different. How is the information given in the website different from the information in this chapter? What information is the same? How do the two sources present information differently?

Elections
www.mycorelibrary.com/political-parties

IMPORTANT DATES

1775–1783

American colonists fight for independence from Great Britain in the American Revolutionary War.

1787

US leaders draft the Constitution.

1791

Alexander Hamilton and his supporters form the Federalist Party.

1854

The Republican Party forms.

1861–1865

The northern Union fights the southern Confederacy in the American Civil War.

1920s

Republican candidates win all three presidential elections.

1792

Thomas Jefferson's supporters form the Republican Party.

1824

The Democratic-Republicans split, forming the Whig party.

1844

The Democratic-Republicans officially change their party's name to the Democratic Party.

1932

Democrat Franklin D. Roosevelt is elected president.

2009

The Tea Party movement begins influencing elections.

2012

Democratic president Barack Obama is reelected.

STOP AND THINK

Tell the Tale

Invent a platform for your own political party. Then write 200 words that tell the story of a candidate from your party campaigning for president. What is he or she worried about? How does that person spread your party's message to voters? Be sure to set the scene, develop a sequence of events, and offer a conclusion.

Surprise Me

Chapter Two describes how political parties formed in the United States. The history of these groups can be interesting and surprising. Which facts about the history of political parties surprised you? Select two or three facts and write a few sentences about each. Why did you find these facts surprising?

Say What?

Studying the government and political parties can mean learning a lot of new vocabulary. Find five words in this book you've never heard before. Use a dictionary to find out what they mean. Then write the meanings in your own words, and use each word in a new sentence.

You Are There

This book discusses a political rally to elect President Barack Obama. Imagine you are attending the rally. What sights and sounds do you experience? How do you feel? Are you excited or nervous? Write a short journal entry describing the rally.

GLOSSARY

ballot
a paper used to vote in elections so people can vote in secret

candidate
someone who is trying to get elected

conservative
in politics, believing in traditional, established policies in government and society

economy
the system of managing money and buying and selling goods in a country

foreign policy
the interactions of one country's government with other countries' governments

ideals
beliefs or ideas

legislators
people who make laws for a country or state

liberal
in politics, supporting laws that encourage social and political change and new ideas

neutral
not taking sides on an issue

tax
money paid to a government to be used for public services, such as roads, schools, and defense

welfare
government programs that help poor and unemployed people pay for basic needs

LEARN MORE

Books

Cunningham, Kevin. *How Political Campaigns and Elections Work*. Minneapolis: Abdo, 2015.

Jackson, Carolyn. *The Election Book: The People Pick a President*. New York: Scholastic, 2012.

Schmidt, Maegan. *The US Constitution and the Bill of Rights*. Minneapolis: Abdo, 2013.

Websites

To learn more about How the US Government Works, visit **booklinks.abdopublishing.com**. These links are routinely monitored and updated to provide the most current information available.

Visit **www.mycorelibrary.com** for free additional tools for teachers and students.

INDEX

ABOUT THE AUTHOR

Stephanie Finne has been working with children's books for more than 12 years. She has written more than 20 books and enjoys helping children learn about new subjects.